I0164979

Purpose *Plus*:
What Really Matters
at Work

Amy Shenot

Copyright © 2017 by Amy Shenot

All rights reserved. This book or any portion thereof may not be reproduced or used in any manner whatsoever without the express written permission of the publisher except for the use of brief quotations in a book review.

Cover design by Jill Zimmerman

ISBN: 0692963278
ISBN-13: 978-0692963272

Cloud 9 Course Design LLC
948 LaPorte Avenue
Fort Collins, CO 80521

Contents

Chapter 1:

Introduction

Most books about work put personal passions first, focusing on purpose. But honing in on the purpose of our work lives can take a while, and work isn't the only outlet for our passions.

The true short stories in this book, about laughable jobs you'll be thankful you never held, get you thinking about purpose *plus* other important considerations at work:

Purpose	What you value, the purpose of your work
Position	What a job entails–the duties and tasks
People	The nature of the people you work with and report to
Place	Where the work takes place
Price	What you will and won't do for pay and other perks

Noting in every job the activities, people, rewards, and other aspects of the workplace you enjoy–as well as anything that leaves you in the fetal position, rocking and mumbling in a corner—will steer you toward purposeful work and away from nervous breakdowns. I just wish I'd paid attention to all of this decades ago, rather than worked as a live-in nurse and in operating rooms despite being squeamish, enlisted in companies where I couldn't toe the bottom line, and repeated many other absentminded mistakes.

This light-hearted yet practical book is meant to make you laugh at me while learning what matters at work to you. Each story includes takeaway lessons and demonstrates how to apply the dimensions of purpose, position, people, place and price to your work life. Although names of people and places were changed to avoid being punched, everything else you are about to read is ridiculously real.

Part A:

Working through College

Entry-level jobs won't fulfill your life's passions or purpose, but they can pay for college and offer valuable experiences and skills needed to find meaningful positions down the road. Every job gives you a chance to explore your purpose, position, people, place and price.

Chapter 2:

Cashier and Stock Girl

On my sixteenth birthday I started working at Cheap Stuff, a discount store a few blocks from home that my stepfather managed. Rumors of favoritism spread when I was hired, and I was determined to prove I was as deserving as any other employee to wear the homely, blaze orange smock with darts too large for me to fill, even in an extra small.

To appreciate this story think back to the 1980's, when every item in a store had a 10-digit stock-keeping unit and price that had to be entered manually by pressing keys on a cash register. Scanning technology didn't revolutionize and add weeks to our lives until years later.

Excelling as a cashier back then meant learning the keys on the cash register by touch, to simultaneously enter numbers and bag merchandise. Madly driven by mind-numbing monotony that could only be overcome with top speed, I got a method for quickly and accurately keying while bagging down to a science. Many customers noticed and sought me out among the twenty aisles of cashiers every time they made their low-priced purchases.

I discovered to my surprise, after developing my

scientific cashiering method, that Cheap Stuff cashiers were randomly tested for speed and accuracy. My manager, Bridget, approached me one quiet day at the store.

> Bridget: You're going to be tested today, Amy. The objective of the test is to enter the stock-keeping units and prices of ten items and come up with the correct total as quickly as possible.
>
> Me: While bagging the merchandise?
>
> Bridget: Uh, no, just enter the numbers.
>
> Me: Are you sure, because the transactions we perform as cashiers require us to put the merchandise in bags, so perhaps a more accurate test would include…
>
> Bridget: JUST enter the numbers.
>
> Me: Got it!

Bridget taped cardboard over the keys on my cash register, requiring me to enter the numbers by touch. I later learned that I held the dubious distinction of being the only cashier in the large Cheap Stuff chain to pass this test in under a minute, to this day my closest claim to fame.

There were the rare entertaining moments at Cheap Stuff when I felt rewarded with breaks from the routine of cashiering. I had fun answering and directing calls that came into the store because I could change my volume or accent every time I spoke over the intercom. A little bit softer now (barely a whisper): "Sporting goods, line one." A little bit louder now, since the store rule was everything had to be repeated (and my rule was everything had to be repeated with a *twist*): "SPORTing Goods, LINE ONE!"

When you're bored at work, what do you do to entertain yourself or create moments of fun? Whatever work you do, find something to laugh about, but avoid making your co-workers the butts of your jokes.

Toward the end of my days at Cheap Stuff, I needed to pull every creative stop to pass the time while stocking shelves from 10pm to 8am. A small crew of janitors swept to country music as I stocked whatever was in the stack of boxes for the night while drowning out the twangy tunes with deep thoughts, such as, *hold it together, everything is temporary, hold it together*. The country music radio station played the same set of sappy songs as I shelved the same item of merchandise, over and over and over.

One night I tripped burglar alarms by opening the wrong exit door, triggering the only sounds to ever drown out the country music, a few sharp words from the boss, and a panic attack every time I'd open an exit door thereafter. Another time someone called the store at closing time to say he'd planted a bomb and I was told to search for it in the stockroom. I obediently complied, shaking while making my way up and down each row of the huge stockroom, listening for anything ticking and looking for anything out of place resembling every other bomb I'd never seen.

During my teenage years at Cheap Stuff I grew and gained weight, eventually filling out the dreaded darts of my extra-small work smock with a padded bra. I can still conjure up the feelings of satisfaction and joy in putting that ugly uniform and the tedium of four years at Cheap Stuff behind me.

Our first instincts can be very telling. What about your first jobs were you most enthusiastic to see behind you? Do you still try to avoid whatever that was in the work you do now? On the other hand and listening to your heart, what did you love about those work experiences, and are you still loving it in your work life today?

Lessons Learned

- Striving to be the best, even at boring tasks, opens doors (but hopefully not alarm-rigged exit doors that trigger panic attacks) to new challenges.
- Make the most of the fun and varied moments that break up monotony at work.

Purpose, Position, People, Place, Price

- I found purpose in overcoming boredom with top speed.

- I improved my position with opportunities to work the phones.
- Interactions with others were brief and impersonal.
- Stores aren't my favorite places.
- I saved and paid for two years of college.

Song Titles Inspired by the Job
- Work IS the Bomb
- Boredom in Blaze Orange Blues

Chapter 3:

Live-in Nurse and Lackey

I needed an affordable place to live independently the summer between my first two years in a college dorm to earn financial aid for the remainder of my studies. What looked like the brightest solution at the time, to find a job with room and board, turned out to be one of the darkest periods of my life.

My best friend, Jess, and I eagerly searched together for jobs that summer as nannies on the east coast, where rich families adore hard-working farmers' daughters from the heartland. One agency that helped families find nannies asked if we'd be live-in's for seniors. We answered *yes* to increase our chance of being hired, and because we were good girls from the Midwest who naturally loved and respected our elders. The agency found a perfect match, a 65-year-old client, Alda, who was looking for a little help around her house and wanted to hire both Jess and me.

We arrived for our first day on the job, expecting to do some light dusting. Alda's daughter, Brenda, picked us up at the airport and launched into indecipherable comments about frequent power outages and where to find nitroglycerin and a generator. We weren't following. Where were the dust rags?

Brenda dropped us off in front of our new home, leaving us with a key and directions to go directly to Alda's bedroom in the back of the house. As we shut the car doors, Brenda sped away.

Jess unlocked the front door and we walked through the musty living room and cramped kitchen, passing a bedroom and bathroom on the left and a dining nook on the right. Opening what we expected to be the door to Alda's bedroom, we stepped through a trick door straight into an intensive care unit, or so it seemed.

I looked around, trying to wake up from a different spin on that nightmare where you're about to sit for a final exam in calculus only to realize that you haven't even cracked open the text. If you've ever experienced anything like this, you've most likely paid attention to the red flags waving before you. Either way, you'll appreciate this story and what happens when you ignore those red flags.

Terrified and unqualified, Jess and I tried to make sense of the patient, equipment, and predicament before us. As a result of polio, Alda's mobility was severely limited and she spent most of her time in bed. She had a tracheostomy and couldn't breathe for any length of time without a ventilator. Jess and I were suddenly round-the-clock nurses, using bedpans, supplies to clean a tracheal tube, and many other items I longed to put aside for another lick on my lollipop.

Alda's physical limitations made us nurses, cooks, housekeepers, groundskeepers, and grocery shoppers. Alda's vanity and our only means to financial aid for college made us hairdressers, makeup artists, personal shoppers, and everything else Alda wanted us to be.

Jess put on a good face and was always pleasant, kind and nurturing. I was neither able to fake a smile nor contain frequent, loud gags that made my eyes water and my face beet red. Undoubtedly you can relate in some way–I mean, come on, right? We're simply not cut out for every job, especially the ones where we lack both the qualifications *and* the aptitude.

One morning I was curling Alda's hair as she talked on the phone about how this was clearly not the job for me. I snuck a tape recorder into the back pocket of Alda's wheelchair, hit the Record button, and started rolling (the tape and Alda's hair). Listening to the recording while drinking Alda's vodka that night gave Jess and me the comic relief we craved. But when the only fun you can find at work comes from a bottle, it might be time to pay attention to those pesky red flags.

Alda would press a bedside button wired to the doorbell when she needed assistance. Bright and early the next morning, Alda summoned me. RING!! RIIIIING!!

Alda: Did you girls get into my liquor cabinet last night?

Me: Oh no, of course not. (In this true story, I'm admitting to telling a white lie.)

Alda: Well, it took a long time for you to wake up and even more time to fix my ventilator.

Me (this is what I must've been thinking, but I don't remember exactly what I said): Yes, you did need to rouse me from a drunken slumber, but pardon me, I'm 18 years old with zero training in life-support equipment repair.

Right after that incident, Jess and I called Shelly, our employment agent, and explained what we were doing on the job. Shelly immediately found us a new assignment and fired Alda, apologizing for a client's dishonesty getting us wrapped up in a lot more than a little help around the house. Beginning with a train trip the next day from Connecticut to New Jersey, Jess and I were off to clean house and help entertain weekend guests for what Shelly described as an "adult couple on the Jersey shore."

We were to be picked up at the train station by the lady of the house, Grace. Imagine our surprise to be greeted by a stunning woman who was only a few years our senior! Jess and I were thrilled to be riding in a red Mercedes convertible to our new home on the beach, where we both laid our landlocked eyes on an ocean for the first time.

Grace pulled into a large garage alongside a matching red Mercedes convertible and we admired the twin set as Jared, the other "adult," helped with our luggage. Imagine our surprise to be greeted by a cunning man who was a senior citizen! Jared was 65 and Grace was 23.

After we met Jared he showed us to the spacious bedroom we'd share and gave us time to unpack and unwind. We hysterically giggled, relieved to be free of Alda, charged to be living in a sweet spot on the shore, and not spoiling the moment with any mention of the dirty words "sugar daddy."

Our jobs were to shop, run other errands, clean, do laundry, and help Grace and Jared entertain friends. During the weekdays we finished our work early and spent carefree afternoons body surfing. On weekends we served meals and cocktails to guests, and we followed them around with a hand-held broom and dustpan to sweep any sand tracked into the house. We kept the house immaculate and the guests served with a wholesome smile.

Some of the adult items we cleaned weren't always pleasant to handle, but everything is relative. Hand wash your dirty lingerie? No problem, I'm grateful to no longer be washing a trachea. And at times, Grace and Jared would get into who knew what behind closed doors and ask us to clean up after them. Scrub the ice cream off the mirrored walls of your bedroom? Whatever, as long as I'm not responsible for whether you live or die.

At first Jess and I thought we had it made. Soon we realized the walls covered in ice cream were just the tip of the iceberg. Jared was brutish, and it was only a matter of time before he lost control of his temper and we lost our jobs.

Grace and Jared shared a bedroom above ours and we began to hear them fighting. Hushed voices of lovers' quarrels crescendoed to harsh words, screams and signs of physical abuse. After a couple of weeks of mistreatment, Grace snuck out in the middle of the night. I wonder what happened to Grace because when she left, she didn't have any money, work experience, or clean lingerie.

In fear of Jared's temper, Jess and I headed back to the Midwest a few weeks earlier than planned. The silver lining was we'd spent enough time on our own to be eligible for financial aid and continue our college studies.

Lessons Learned
- Take action quickly (get help or get out) if you realize you're in a position way over your head.
- A beautiful work setting is a lovely perk (and a potential ruse).

Purpose, Position, People, Place, Price

- I purposefully earned financial aid to stay in college.
- Most of the duties were disgusting, demeaning, or both.
- I'm definitely not cut out for nursing or doting on people.
- Live-in employment wasn't for me, but livin' on the coast was sweet.
- I paid a huge price just to earn financial aid, but that did pay off.

Song Titles Inspired by the Job

- Alda's Ventilator
- Red Flags, White Lies, and Blue Bloods

Chapter 4:

Receptionist and Security Guard

At long last, I had financial aid that included funding toward a "work-study position," and I was off to the financial aid office to find a job from the list of work-to-study-to-no-longer-need-these positions. The job that stood out was with Contemporary Art Museum. Working reception at a downtown museum just two blocks from my apartment sounded ideal, and I was honored to be hired.

I developed useful administrative and technical skills working in the museum office as a receptionist, database administrator, and coordinator of a large art fair. Sitting at the front desk and talking with patrons and colleagues made me feel part of a community, as well as much more sophisticated than I ever did in an orange smock with saggy darts.

Just as reception and other work around the museum office was starting to get old, the Gallery Operations Manager offered me a promotion to security guard. Security was the best job for college students working at the museum because we had a quiet place to study. As guards, we were responsible for setting alarms and locking doors to close and secure the galleries. While the galleries were open, all we had to do was make sure visitors didn't touch or take pictures of the art. That left plenty of time to do my homework *and* the homework for the guy I was "dating." (I called it "dating." He called it "getting his homework done." Semantics.)

The Gallery Operations Manager, who answered only to "GOM" and secretly wished for the title of Gallery Operations Director, thought he was GOM's gift to women. Despite being fat, short, and bald with yellow teeth and coffee breath, GOM hit on every woman that worked at Contemporary Art Museum, convinced we were all wildly attracted to him.

> GOM: You very much want to kiss me right now, don't you, Amy.
> Me: No, GOM, I really don't.
> GOM: But you think longingly about kissing me often, don't you, Amy.
> Me: No, I've never thought of kissing you. Quit thinking and saying that I do, and consider mints, please. Thank you, GOM.

The art galleries were on multiple levels, each with at least one guarding station. We took turns at the stations and became familiar with every exhibit. When we were done with our homework we played games on our walkie talkies, weapons that made us a force to be reckoned with when serious security duties called.

As I was locking up one night I had to use my walkie talkie for real, to call for backup. Out of the corner of my eye I saw a man behind a column in the gallery upstairs. My colleague came running as soon as he got my call, along with others who couldn't contain their laughter. The curator and installation crew had planned a publicity stunt and I was their pawn. The man I thought I saw was a piece of artwork in a new exhibit featuring lifelike statues, and the next day a local newspaper article promoted the exhibit as having statues so realistic even a security guard at the museum was duped.

Contemporary Art Museum hosts a huge annual art fair. As part of the security team at the art fair I drove a golf cart to collect and move money from the museum's booths to the bank. My fellow guards and I turned this into a game by divvying up the booths, starting at the same time, and racing to our booths and the bank. Then we'd count the money together and drive our carts, pedal to the metal, to the closest bar for a Bloody Mary. We repeated this run every couple of hours. Racing golf carts in a large crowd was tricky at the beginning of those days and should've put us behind bars by the end.

Before I graduated and left my university town to

enter the real world, I had a second security position for a few months in the School of Music, where I swapped student I.D.'s for practice room keys. These practice rooms were the best kept secret on campus, a free place you could use to privately make sweet music behind locked doors. My job duties for the music school also included walking the halls and locking the building after hours.

The times have changed a lot, or perhaps I'm just overlooking the skinny, unarmed, untrained, young women policing and securing large buildings late at night. And that's a crying shame, for security was the perfect gig for this college girl with keys that opened doors to art and music.

Lessons Learned

- The best bosses and colleagues create a stimulating workplace.
- Many jobs are right for a period of time but not for a lifetime. (Working security was fitting during my studies but would bore me to tears under other circumstances. You may hold jobs that you wouldn't want to keep forever yet are right at the time, like Mr. Right Now, the boyfriend who is fine for a while but not husband material.)
- Sometimes a job is simply a means to support yourself as you work toward a college degree or other

credential.

Purpose, Position, People, Place, Price

- Doing my homework at work was purposeful.
- I was promoted to the best position for college students.
- The people I worked with were fun and friendly.
- The museum and music school offered new cultural opportunities.
- I earned decent wages for easy work.

Song Titles Inspired by the Job

- Booths and Banks and Bloodies–Oh My!
- Keys to Culture and Love

Part B:

Dabbling in Different Jobs

There may be frustrating times in your work life when you lack clear purpose. Turning your attention to the other dimensions (position, people, place and price) is both comforting and useful toward finding better work in the future. Maybe you'll discover what matters to you most is to be with a certain population of people or to spend your days in a natural setting. Coming to such conclusions will clarify your purpose.

Chapter 5:

Retail Manager

Four years at Cheap Stuff convinced me I never wanted to work in retail again. The opportunity to live in warmer climes and the only offer on the table when I was graduating from college in debt forced me to reconsider. Out of necessity, I accepted a management position with an upscale retailer in Florida.

My college roommate, Carla, encouraged me to apply for a job at Upscale Retailer when she heard any applicant to make the third and final round of interviews would get to go on a free cruise. We both participated in the first two rounds of interviews and anticipated a fun trip together. Lucky for her, by not advancing in the selection process, Carla avoided a bad trip. She did, however, miss a fabulous cruise.

Florida looks like the Promised Land when you're from the heartland and need a light box to ward off seasonal affective disorder. Dread of the impending doom of long, cold, grey winters would set in every year around Labor Day and I'd be wearing a hat 24/7 by Halloween, until May Day. Visions of palm trees, sandy beaches, gulf waters, and both halves of the year without hat head made it impossible to imagine one more brutal winter. Although I knew retail management wasn't my calling, I accepted Upscale Retailer's offer, reminded myself everything is temporary, and focused on how much I love to swim outdoors.

At my Upscale Retailer store I withstood long hours managing four departments and 50 sales associates, who were required to meet sales quotas to keep their jobs. Every employee used a unique number to track sales. I hated firing people, so when nobody was looking, I'd ring up sales using the numbers of associates falling behind. Magically, everyone in my departments made their quotas. The ten-key skills I developed over the years at Cheap Stuff came right back to help this hack be nimble, hack be quick.

I did a lot of things at Upscale Retailer when nobody was looking, and I encouraged the sales associates I managed to follow my lead. Another job requirement for associates was to find customers who wanted personal-shopping experiences, a doting clerk to select and accessorize fashionable outfits just for them. Monitoring whether associates were meeting their requirements as personal shoppers was up to each manager and on the honor system. The best approach was to take advantage of the honor system with a notepad I kept behind me in my office, where associates logged whatever they wanted, knowing nobody was looking.

My job did require enough thought to keep me sane,

such as identifying which clothing cuts and colors were trendy. But mostly I walked the floors of the store and made sure customers were well served and associates well behaved.

When I needed a change of pace, namely from walking to standing, I rode up and down on the escalators in the middle of the store for panoramic views of my departments and relief from foot pain. Riding the escalators was also the only way to fully avoid the competing scents from the perfume counters below and the chemicals wafting from the hair salon above.

A formal dress code ruled out walking shoes, the only kind of shoe I can wear comfortably on my gimpy feet. Eileen, my micro manager, sent me home to change clothes one day, claiming I was "dressed for a picnic" when I tried to get away with boxy-toed shoes and a sweater rather than tight dress shoes and a tailored jacket. Eileen was absolutely right about one thing: working at Upscale Retailer was no picnic. In retrospect, wearing a blaze orange smock every day at work was terrific–the smock matched perfectly with my comfy sneakers.

After a few months I knew walking relentless floors day after day in dress shoes was unsustainable, so I started looking for another job. Eileen caught wind of my job search from a co-worker I thought was a friend and called me into her office.

Eileen: Kathy tells me you're looking for other work. Are you able to put your heart into this job, or should I be asking for your letter of resignation?

Me: I will put my heart into the job. (What else could I say with my back up against the wall?)

And I did put my heart into the job by protecting the people I managed from being fired. What I could no longer put into the job were my aching feet, shrinking mind, and trust in co-workers.

I told Eileen what she needed to hear so I could pay the bills and continued to look for other work. About a week later I found a new job and gave two weeks' notice of my resignation to Upscale Retailer. A week after that, the regional manager for Upscale Retailer, Big Wig, was scheduled to visit the store.

In the world of retail management, department managers live in fear of store managers, who live in fear of district managers, with every manager needing hefty doses of anti-anxiety medication for the rare regional manager's visit. During my final days at Upscale Retailer, when I should've been reveling in the bliss of short-timer status, I was bossed around more than ever. Eileen constantly reminded me to have plenty of my most knowledgeable sales associates ready for the important visit ahead.

As we were opening the store on the big day of Big Wig's arrival, Eileen counted the number of sales associates in my departments. In her opinion, which I was so over having to accept as fact, there weren't enough. So Eileen ordered me to pretend I was a sales associate in the sunglasses kiosk.

Big Wig normally asked several questions of one or two associates selected randomly from hundreds in the store. When the store visit began and I saw Big Wig guide Eileen to me, I snuck her a pair of sunglasses to hide the look of fear in her eyes.

I was a loose cannon; Eileen had been controlling and unkind. How would I answer Big Wig's questions? Would I seize this improbable opportunity for revenge while on my way out, with nothing to lose? I wish I could give you more, but at this point in my life I was finally starting to mature. Rather than put Eileen in her place as she delighted in doing to me, I respectfully answered every question, impressed Big Wig with my knowledge and customer service, and never revealed I was a manager in disguise behind all those sunglasses, about to pick up my last paycheck and walk out the door for the last time.

Lessons Learned
- If you're in a line of work and don't like it, you

probably won't like being in that line of work again.

- No free lunch? In the world of work, there's no free cruise, either.
- Some people thrive and excel in positions of authority, and others (myself included) don't.

Purpose, Position, People, Place, Price

- The sole purpose was to pay the bills.
- The duties for this position were painful.
- My boss was intolerable and my co-workers were untrustworthy.
- A place with warmer weather was welcomed.
- Given the low salary and long hours, I paid a big price to pay the bills.

Song Titles Inspired by the Job

- Dressed for Pain
- Sunglasses of Fear
- Free Cruise Comeuppance

Chapter 6:

Account Executive

Desperate to make Upscale Retailer a speck in my rearview mirror, I applied to be the receptionist for a local media lab, Presentations Matter. In the 1980's you could buy a used car in mint condition for what you'd pay Presentations Matter to produce the film slides and provide the equipment and services you needed to give a professional presentation. Technology has come a long way, making it free and easy today for everyone to underwhelm us everywhere with homespun digital slideshows.

The owner of Presentations Matter, Greg, called after interviewing me for the job. Our conversation went something like this:

Greg: I have good news and bad news. Which do you want first?

Me: The bad news.

Greg: We hired someone else to be our receptionist.

Me: OK...what's the good news?

Greg: The good news is we want to expand our marketing department and offer you a better position, Account Executive, with a higher salary plus commissions.

Me: Absolutely, thank you so much, I'll take it!

Without pause I accepted Greg's offer and started the job, relieved to be done with retail management and sure I'd be earning a fortune now that I was an executive. During my first few weeks on the job I watched presentations and served as a stage hand, appreciating Greg's bottom-up approach to executive training while quietly wondering whether I'd be offered a top-floor office with a bay or skyline view.

Every year Presentations Matter's top client, Ham, spent enough on slideshows to buy a fleet of gently used cars. During my training I helped Ham with his most theatrical production, performed in a stately conference ballroom and featuring diamonds he'd award his top salesmen. Ham hired a sexy woman from a talent agency for the starring role, directing her to seductively saunter across the stage and through the crowd with a platter of perfect gems.

The talent didn't show, but Ham insisted the show must go on. Greg unbuttoned the top buttons of my blouse, handed me the platter, opened the stage curtains, and cast me in the role of a sexy woman. Although Greg's training methods were unorthodox, I was learning how to act quickly, take on challenging roles, and deflect the heat when all eyes were on me–useful skills for any executive. That said, was the takeaway lesson supposed to be nobody makes it to the top by buttoning up?

Slowly I pieced together that my job responsibilities weren't nearly as glamorous as my job title. I'd been hired to sell slides to actual executives from a small, shared office on the ground floor with a view of the parking lot.

Convinced I wasn't cut out for selling anything, I bought time by researching prospective clients. Greg valued and used my marketing research, making me happy to give something back for his investment in me.

Without a doubt, what came next–making cold calls to these prospective clients–was my most gut-wrenching work task *ever*. On the rare occasions I was able to get past a receptionist to speak with an executive, I was too dumbfounded to initiate, let alone close, sales. Although I eventually made and delivered brochures with sample slides, replacing each cold call with a warm welcome, from my first attempts to sell slides the outcome was clear: I'd never be hot.

I wasn't a successful or happy salesperson or Florida resident. So I said goodbye to my days of outdoor swimming when I wasn't selling slides or trendy clothes and drove across the country with a friend for a fresh start.

Lessons Learned

- Job titles can be euphemisms.
- Not all tasks are included in job descriptions. (For example, provocatively working a room of men didn't appear in mine.)
- When performing a job ties your stomach in knots and leaving it fills you with relief, find another line of work and never look back.
- Add value before you move on when you suspect you will be a short-timer, particularly when an employer is investing in you.

Purpose, Position, People, Place, Price

- I developed marketable communication and presentation skills.
- Sales is definitely not for me.
- Connecting and socializing with smart, creative peers was fulfilling.
- Working in a lab and on stage had its moments.
- The pay was OK, the learning experience priceless.

Song Titles Inspired by the Job

- Hard Sell Slides
- Diamonds Aren't a Girl's Best Friend

Chapter 7:

Temp, Office Manager, Temp Again

The day after making the long drive from Florida to Washington for a fresh start, I applied at a temporary employment agency for the first time. Like every other temp my aim was to sneak in through the back door with a temporary position that would lead to a permanent job. I had no clue what I wanted that permanent job to be, but I was determined to land it. The ten-key wizardry I'd mastered at Cheap Stuff wowed the placement agents and moved me to the front of the line for riveting data-entry opportunities.

My first assignment was with a giant in computer software. I applied from within for a fantastic job that would've been mine if it weren't for my petty supervisor at this company, who'd been overlooked for similar positions and spitefully lied about my performance. I needed her recommendation to be hired for a permanent position. After spending months that crawled by like decades entering data and falling into a deep tedium-induced trance, it was time to wake up, wipe the drool off my chin, and face another job search.

The trouble is I've never put much effort into job searches. Apparently I don't like selling myself any more than I liked selling slides. Back in 1989 I reached yet again for the low-hanging fruit of an ad: a media lab similar to Presentations Matter was looking for an office manager. My daunting job search was over after placing one phone call and participating in one short interview, where I accepted one terribly low offer.

The upshot was that working at Slide Productions was interesting, and every aspect of my job short of the paycheck grew rapidly. I loved doing anything *but* sales. On an average day I'd bookkeep, storyboard presentations, talk to clients, develop film, and manage many projects and deadlines.

There were only three of us at Slide Productions: Jack the owner, Jill the sales manager, and me. When I arrived one day to find Jack and Jill whispering behind closed doors, I knew they weren't scheming how to share the news of my pay going uphill. It was the opposite; Jack was planning to retire and close shop.

Unable to stomach another job search but still in debt, back I went to the temp agency and back I was working with numbers, in the treasury department of a gas utility. Lisa, my co-worker at Blue Flame, treated me as an equal. She taught me how to determine the amount to invest or borrow at the end of each day and to make electronic transfers of funds in millions of dollars. We collaborated on elaborate spreadsheets and financial statements.

On the flip side, Donna, my supervisor, had me escort her to meetings carrying her coffee, briefcase and flip chart. Donna was the only female executive, expected to be treated like a princess, and made me her personal Cinderella. One minute I'd be transferring millions of dollars for Lisa and the next I'd be erasing Donna's chalkboard.

> Donna (yelling to me at a desk ten feet outside of her office): Amy, the sun is getting in my eyes. Come to my office and close my blinds.
> Me: Coming, Donna, I'll be right there for you.
> Donna (raising her empty mug while I close her blinds): Then go to the kitchen and get me some coffee with cream and sugar.
> Me: On my way, Donna, I'll be right back for you.
> Donna: And when you return, close my door and answer my calls.
> Me: Of course, Donna, I'm always here for you.

Most days at Blue Flame the hardest work I faced was practicing patience with Princess Donna. At least I got to later commiserate with Lisa when called upon to do whatever drudgery Donna deemed beneath her and wanted others to see her *not* doing through the glass walls of her office.

Working as a temp and taking what felt like an eternity to find my work purpose really brought me down. I got serious about analyzing my work life. As you reflect on your work life you can use the process of elimination to hone in on the responsibilities, people, work environments and perks that do and don't suit you. Thinking back on my past jobs revealed much of what I would and wouldn't like about any future job.

If only in your teens you could ride a time machine fifty years into the future, then return to your younger self with all the knowledge needed to pave and set out on your ideal career path. Wisdom is gained in the real world only through the passage of real time; however, you can significantly shorten and ease the pain of the process of elimination by contemplating in every job your purpose, position, people, place and price!

Around the same time my overdue and deep career reflection began, I started volunteering in a center for student services at a community college. There I instantly felt at home in a way I never had in any other work setting. I loved helping advisors guide students to courses and careers. The more I learned from the advisors the more I was able to apply insights to my own work prospects, leading me to explore careers and graduate degrees in education.

Finding my purpose was a long, messy process. I

believe only the lucky people, those born knowing what they 'want to be when they grow up,' get to skip the trying aspects of discovery. In today's work world with so many choices, muddled work paths are the new normal.

After wearing out my wellies from so much mucking around I applied for and was accepted into a master's degree program in higher education, but my studies wouldn't begin for several months. I needed to save money for school and myself from job hunting with an increase in my slave wages.

Me: Hello, I'd like to discuss a raise for my assignment at Blue Flame. My supervisor here wants me to stay until I move away in June.

Temp Agent: Our temps don't decide how much they make or how long they stay! WE tell YOU what to do!

Me: Actually, I am letting you decide. You can continue to earn half the amount you currently make for the hours I work and pay the other half to me, or I'll quit, and you'll make nothing *and* lose a client.

That one business course in negotiations I slept through after graveyard shifts at Cheap Stuff made me think I had power to wield. I got the raise and endured another few months as a temp entrusted with multimillion-dollar decisions, confident I'd made a smart move in choosing a graduate degree and career in higher education.

Lessons Learned

- Look out for yourself in competitive work environments.
- You earn bargaining power by proving your worth.
- Variety is the spice of life, and learning new knowledge and skills at work is motivating.

Purpose, Position, People, Place, Price

- The main purpose was to stimulate reflection, leading to better work choices.
- Temporary grunt work is just that, but the variety of duties as an office manager was great.
- The people were OK but nobody lit my fire.
- I liked working in a darkroom and in a small office.
- This has to be the last set of gigs that are just about paying the bills, right?

Song Titles Inspired by the Job

- Temp Slave
- Corporate Slave
- Donna's Slave

Chapter 8:

Instructor and Research Assistant

At age 25 I was studying education and sure I was on the right track, a wide track with all lanes leading to good jobs in higher education and none returning to slave labor. Student services, teaching, curriculum development, and research all interested me. I chose the fast lane of student services, with a master's degree I began one summer and finished the next.

Although the first summer term of my degree program was the most demanding, going to school without having to work was like an extended holiday. I'd saved enough money and found a cheap room for the summer to enjoy this delicious taste of freedom and lots of outdoor swimming.

Late in the summer I found a job listing to teach "Introduction to Library Science" in the coming Fall, Winter, and Spring trimesters. Reading the fine print, I learned that four course sections of 30 students each were offered every trimester, and if hired, I'd be given a syllabus but otherwise need to consult a Magic 8 Ball for answers on how to effectively teach the course.

I desperately applied, thinking my chances were as slim as my dwindling savings. I had no teaching experience, the professor who'd normally oversee a teaching assistant would be overseas, and the potential for so many disgruntled students and parents was risky for the university. Perhaps I was the only one foolish enough to apply after summing up the situation: this was a big job for little pay. I didn't care. I wanted the experience, I got it, and the autonomy was refreshing. In fact, I loved everything about teaching and still do, with the exception of repetitive grading.

My students and I spent most class periods in the campus library getting hands-on practice with reference books, the card catalog (yes, that dates me *almost* as much as talking about film slides), and CD-ROM's (another obsolete method of searching for information).

Me: Today we're going to learn how to use the card catalog. How would you find the book "The Joy of Sex" using the card catalog?

Member of Class: I'd look up the title, under "J."

Another Member of Class: I'd search by author.

Me: Great! Anyone else? (Pause, silence.) You mean to tell me you haven't searched for the joy of sex in the library? (Giggles.) What's special about the card catalog is every topic has a unique call number, so you can find everything about it....

After introducing the lessons and providing a brief demonstration, I'd help students find library resources and feel like I had the most awesome job in the world. That attitude of gratitude did go south when it came time to grade, though. Repeatedly grading almost any assignment is tiresome, and if you agree, don't assign lengthy annotated bibliographies to 360 students.

In addition to my teaching position, I was relieved to find another job as a research assistant starting in the Fall trimester. After swimming all summer, it was time to double down. In my second job I was a grant administrator and edited a curriculum-development guide for vocational educators. I was immediately drawn to curriculum development.

By the time I finished graduate school, I'd explored academic and career advising, teaching, grant administration, curriculum development, scholarly research, and the 20th-century science of library card catalogs. My job settings and relationships with college and university colleagues were also proving positive, a welcome change from stifling workplaces with slave-driving bosses and self-serving co-workers. Soon I'd discover, after many years of working without clear purpose, how this one fruitful year had launched me on the right track.

Lessons Learned

- When you find a line of work that's right for you, you will know–it just feels right.
- Lifelong learning is important at work, home, and anywhere else you want to thrive.

Purpose, Position, People, Place, Price

- I enthusiastically explored multiple purposes in higher education.
- The autonomy of teaching was wonderful.
- I valued working on a small research team with bright people.
- Working at a university felt right.
- Paying my way through graduate school while developing a variety of skills was perfect.

Song Titles Inspired by the Job

- Magic 8 Ballin' It
- Fast Lane to Freedom

Chapter 9:

Temp for the Last Time

Soon after finishing my graduate degree, I was back in the heartland with a plan to work at my beloved alma mater, University of the Heartland (UH). Until I found a job at UH I needed to temp. I found another data-entry position where I could impress a temp agency's client with my record-breaking speed. This time, my experience working security also played into my placement.

My agent at the temp agency told me my job would be to keep the books for a local distributor while their bookkeeper, Anne, was on maternity leave. After two weeks of training, I'd be working alone and locking up at night.

My mood lifted when I pulled into the distributor's parking lot for my first day of work and saw the rows of trucks plastered with beer advertisements and loaded with alcohol; this could be an intoxicating gig after all. As I made my way to the office, I spotted a warehouse full of beer, a staff kitchen full of beer drinkers, and a shadow full of Anne down the hallway.

Her silhouette gave her away and when we met, I had to bite my tongue from asking how many babies she was expecting. She looked to be 13 months pregnant with sextuplets. Anne shared her frustration over the managers not bringing me onboard at least two months, rather than only two weeks, before little Aaron, Andy, Alicia, Adrian, Alexis and Ashley were due. Wanting to keep the blood pressure of these seven beings where it should be, I assured Anne I had loads of experience cleaning up after my own and others' mistakes, and we began my crash training course without delay.

I quickly figured out that Anne was the only person at the distributor who knew the computer-based bookkeeping system; the first thing Anne taught me was *not* to teach anyone else how to do anything she was teaching me. She was the only person who knew how to enter daily information from the drivers, including how many cases of beer were delivered, sold and returned. If you worked at the beer distributor and had a question about anything related to numbers or counting (not accounting, just counting), Anne made sure she was the only person with the answer. Some people love control, and when it came to her babies and the beer distributor's books, Anne was large and in charge.

But nature decided for Anne that her little ones would arrive early, and she went into labor the second day I was on the job. We had hardly scratched the surface of tracking returned cases of beer when her contractions began.

Anne had to be pulled out of the office as she panted final words about Driver Ivan, bad at counting (yet surprisingly good at accounting), and Driver Dale, whose returned cases usually ended up down his throat.

The managers scrambled when Anne left the building. Would the enterprise crumble, a jumble of numbers and miscounted merchandise? I'd been around the work block enough times to recognize control freaks and the tricks they play to exaggerate their importance. Remember Eileen, my micro manager at Upscale Retailer? We all have these controlling characters in our lives. Confident in my experience with computers, bookkeeping, and cleaning up all manners of messes, I thought, *how hard could it be?*

You might be expecting to find the situation turned out to be comically difficult or tragic, that Driver Ivan wasn't the only one losing count or Driver Dale wasn't the only one losing consciousness. But while the managers scrambled, I reassured them everything would be fine *if* I tried really, really hard. I set out to make myself as needed as Anne, then paid as much.

Shortly thereafter, I found a fantastic position in student services at the University of the Heartland (UH). The new job wouldn't begin until after Anne returned, and I was in a bargaining position with both the beer distributor and the temp agency.

Beer Boss: Yes, Amy, what is it you wanted to talk

about?

Me: I just accepted a job at UH, but I could continue to work here until Anne returns, if needed.

Beer Boss: Why yes, thank you, only the two of you know the complex computer system.

Me: Right… and I think it's fair to say I'm not being compensated enough for that. All I ask is for more from the temp agency of what you're already paying them, and I'd be happy to contact my agent with this request.

Beer Boss: We will fire the temp agency and hire you. How much do you want?

Of course, I don't remember the exact words of these conversations, but you get the idea. I had a beer distributor over a barrel, which made it possible for me to take it easy and drink free beers before getting all adult-like with my job at UH.

On my last night as a lonely bookkeeper, I locked the doors one last time and drove away, making a pact with myself to never need to temp or do any other kind of grunt work again, yearning for those desperado days to be over for good. Happily that moment was the last time I had to stoop to uninspiring work to survive. Don't despair if you haven't yet reached such a turning point in your work life. The road can be long and winding, but one day you will arrive.

Lessons Learned

- Opportunities to demonstrate your worth and negotiate outcomes favorable to all parties come up in many jobs.
- If you have your employer over a barrel, use that power judiciously.
- Some people are control freaks, so some people at work are bound to be control freaks, too.

Purpose, Position, People, Place, Price

- Once again, my main purpose was survival.
- I was reminded that repetitive tasks are deadly.
- Working alone while co-workers drank beer got old.
- A place with free beer is not entirely lacking.
- Shortly after proving my worth, I negotiated a raise.

Song Titles Inspired by the Job

- Bottomless Bottles
- Drunk Driver Dale

Part C:

Finding Fitting Work

Being aware of and keeping a balanced perspective about all of the dimensions at work will help you stay upbeat during times when finding work with "purpose *plus*" is challenging. The more you learn about your needs and desires on the job, the more fitting work you'll be able to find.

Chapter 10:

Associate Director of Education

After 16 years of work trials and errors, starting with six long years of babysitting, I had lasting, meaningful work and a good salary. In addition to loving the novel sensation of extra pocket change, I was instantly hooked on having a big, ever-changing role on a small team, to this day my favorite dynamic.

I joined a handful of staff and interns dedicated to continuously improving UH's first distance-learning degree program, and we all had big roles. Being the first to do anything at an institution of UH's size and snail's pace meant we had to fight every battle tooth and nail, and if at first we did not succeed, try, try again with another bureaucrat. We weren't reinventing the wheel, we were blazing the trail and pushing the envelope, even though we knew bureaucrats prefer to push pencils.

The technology of the day allowed us to deliver the degree program to remote learners in ways your great, great grandparents would've never dreamed possible. Bulky desktop computers, printers, fax machines, telephones, the United States postal service, and short residencies on campus to begin and end courses made it possible for doctors to become healthcare administrators without moving to campus or leaving their jobs. In the early 1990's, this method of instructional delivery was revolutionary. I remember telling my friend, Jackie, that I'd happened upon the field of distance education, and Jackie asking, "Does that mean the chalkboard is farther from the desks?" Now when asked what I do for a living I simply say I create and teach online courses, and people nod in instant recognition.

The early days of the Internet brought exciting opportunities for my colleagues and me to be pioneers on the new frontier of online teaching and learning. Today, learning-management systems make it easy to produce and advance masses of learners through online courses. In the 1990's, my team had to cobble together and learn how to use and support a variety of rudimentary online tools that weren't always sharp or able to get along in the tool shed. In other words, the technology wasn't stable, robust, or integrated, so my team had to be all three.

By the early 1990's our program for administrator-wannabe doctors became UH's first degree offered online. My duties swiftly expanded from providing student services to developing the curriculum, courses, and use of instructional technologies.

Email was a new method of communication and instructional technology. In my early days of using email, I composed the message below to a friend, then accidentally sent it to a full class of students.

Hi Sarah.

Sorry I can't join you for dinner. I have to attend a work reception tonight, where the doctors will find out Laura will be taking over as interim director. This is going to go over like a bomb. They already think they're on a sinking ship.

Anyway, see you soon!

Amy

After hitting the "Send" button I received confirmation that my message was successfully sent to "Class of '93." WHAAA??? Didn't I select "Sarah" from my email distribution list?!? My heart raced as I dragged myself to Laura's office to confess what I'd done and beg for her forgiveness before any of the students figured out how to forward the message to her first.

Me (voice trembling): Excuse me, Laura. I'm sorry, I need to tell you about something stupid I just did.

Laura: What is it *this* time?

Me: I sent a message intended for one of my friends to our Class of '93, and I said things I shouldn't have. Please read the message and tell me what I can do to right this wrong.

Laura (after reading the message): Here's what you'll do. Right NOW. You'll send this message. Sit down and begin with this apology.

I did just as Laura dictated, word-for-word, and sent a groveling apology and explanation that made me look even more flighty and presented Laura in a strong yet compassionate light. If you've never had to eat crow in this manner, count your chickens before they hatch.

On the heels of my email blunder, I was shocked and flattered when Laura asked me to run the program as her associate director. Reluctant to turn down this promotion but interested only in certain aspects of the offer, I asked if I could be associate director of education and if my co-worker, Gilda, could be associate director of student services. Remember that lesson I learned about *not* thriving on authority? Whether you like and are good at managing others is an important consideration. I knew supervising Gilda and a couple other team members I nudged her way would've tried my patience. More to the point, I was ready to focus on curriculum development, the lane of the higher-education track that kept me in the zone.

During the last two years on this job, as my team expanded our online offerings and presence at UH, I remember thinking I'd be perfectly happy if what I was doing then would prove to be the pinnacle of my career. I loved being on the bleeding edge and I was instantly–and remain to this day–energized by designing instruction and collaborating with smart, talented instructors.

Tasks that keep us interested, challenged, and motivated to improve are important to seek and, for many of us, rare and hard to find. Be sure to pay attention and take note anytime you find them.

Lessons Learned
- Being on the forefront is exciting and challenging.
- Concentrate on work that puts you 'in the zone.'
- Bureaucracies or any workplaces slow to change can be frustrating, especially if you want to innovate.

Purpose, Position, People, Place, Price
- I stayed in a purposeful zone as a team leader and instructional designer.
- Managing a small team and developing online courses was rewarding.
- My team rocked.
- Working at my alma mater was fun.
- Earning a professional salary while building expertise was very satisfying.

Song Titles Inspired by the Job

- Ballad from the Bleeding Edge
- Drats, More Bureaucrats

Chapter 11:

Outreach Program Manager

When Laura retired and an overbearing director took over I found a new job at UH in the outreach office of the School of Education. Thrilled to accomplish my goal of getting a job in the highly rated school, I couldn't wait to start working with other educators in a majestic, old building at the heart of campus. I'd arrived, or so I thought.

As is the case with many large research universities, research reigns supreme at UH, followed at a distant second by teaching, with outreach being a chore faculty do only after being scolded repeatedly by their mothers. I learned this the hard way by taking on the role of a scolding mother, and what I'd suspected as a babysitter was confirmed: I don't have enough patience to be a parent.

My job was to find instructors willing to teach online in a school firmly gripped by fear of online education. Dean Kaushon, in charge of educational technology for the school and the leading voice on educational technology at UH, gave stern lectures across campus about the need for teaching and learning to occur in a physical space.

He warned faculty to steer clear of the newfangled,

unproven online methods. Following a dean on blind faith was so much easier for faculty than learning to use technology, and in a university hierarchy, a reputable dean has a lot more clout and control than a scolding mother.

I was both a new employee trying to promote online teaching and a recently admitted student in the School of Education. Unfortunately, Dean Kaushon was assigned as my advisor. He "advised" students interested in online education by quenching our thirst for knowledge with his education-only-works-in-physical-spaces Kool Aid. I steered clear of his cult, convinced there was a rightful place for online learning.

My boss and I set out on the only path to progress by infiltrating the dean's office, to change and open minds from the top down. Dean Kaushon blocked our efforts and stood tall, a fortress for face-to-face instruction, but his arguments were losing ground, a sand castle in the rising tide of online education.

Dean Kaushon didn't want minds to change or open. This was the School of Education, after all. He played defense by telling his wife I'd be perfect for an opening at her company, Teams Work. His wife called me, and although the company name alone should've set off alarm bells in my head louder than the imaginary ones I've heard since opening the wrong exit door in the middle of the night at Cheap Stuff, the opportunity to join Teams Work was tempting on many levels.

For one, being surrounded by naysayers is depressing and discouraging. Who needs that much negativity? For another, nobody on my UH work team had a sense of humor. I searched tirelessly behind many elbow patches on tweed jackets but never found a single funny bone.

I was also growing weary of work that was at the bottom of everyone's priority list. The slow, grinding gears of a massive bureaucracy were keeping me down.

By the time the official offer came from Teams Work I was itching to be an integral part of a team that had fun together. As it turned out, Ms. Kaushon and I had very different definitions of "integral" and "fun," but I trusted her take as an insider and enlisted in her company.

Imagine working in a place that lacks your vision, where your spark is snuffed and people are boring and afraid of change. Then one day you hear from an employer, recruiting you for an exciting, lucrative position on a fun, innovative team. How much more would you need to know? (This isn't a rhetorical question. What I should've thought of then is to always get as much information as you can, no matter how good the opportunity sounds.)

Lessons Learned
- Being an integral part of a fun team is motivating.

- Naysayers are nincompoops.
- Over time, doing work that's low on everyone's priority list becomes trying and disheartening.

Purpose, Position, People, Place, Price

- My purpose was thwarted at every turn.
- It's hard to thrive in a position set up for failure by the leadership, or lack of it.
- The people were scared of change and dull, dull, dull.
- The beautiful building and setting I loved as an outsider left me cold within.
- For me, any job this much like sales comes with a price.

Song Titles Inspired by the Job

- Kaushon Kool Aid
- Funny-Boneless Chickens

Chapter 12:

Process Champion

I'd worked at UH for over seven years before I was recruited by Teams Work, a small consulting firm. As a change seeker, the dream of leaving a plodding bureaucracy for fast-paced beginnings overshadowed any memories of working in the business world. How quickly Teams Work reminded me I'm not cut out for corporate cultures.

Six Sigma, an approach to quality management and process improvement, was all the rage. Much of what I did at Teams Work was design presentations used to teach corporate leaders how to implement Six Sigma. Even the phrases "quality management" and "process improvement" give me the willies, let alone "Six Sigma," whatever that means. I wrote a course on Six Sigma and I still don't know.

My corporate-phrase-revulsion meter spiked at 11 the first time I heard over the intercom, "Everyone, please gather in the All-One-Team room." Was this a joke, and was it okay to crouch down behind my cubicle's partition wall to hide the smirk on my face? But this was for real. "All-One-Team" was not only the name of our meeting room, it was how we were to behave and the mission we were to follow with every corporate fiber of our team-building beings.

My working title at Teams Work was Instructional Designer. In both educational and corporate settings, instructional designers play a behind-the-scenes role in designing and producing instructional plans, activities, and materials. Even thoughtful teachers of courses masterfully created by instructional designers show little appreciation for the work. All of that to say I wasn't surprised when the Six Sigma trainer at Teams Work shared her candid thoughts about my role within days of my arrival:

> Lydia: If the team were stranded in our all-one-team lifeboat, you would be the first person I'd throw overboard.
>
> Me: I'm sorry you feel that way. May I ask why?
>
> Lydia: Instructional designers make the least valuable contribution to the team.
>
> Me: Perhaps you've never worked with a good instructional designer. (What I wanted to say was she ought to roll overboard well before me because she weighed at least three times as much, but remarkably, I kept my least-valuable ideas to myself.)

About a month into this job, I was asked by the owner of Teams Work if I'd be her "process champion for creating intellectual capital with market value." Strip away the corporate jargon and this translates to, "Will you efficiently make training courses that sell?" Sure, I nodded as I kept my real thoughts to myself: *I'll only be championing the process of creating intellectual capital for you while I'm on the market in search of a job I value.*

About a year prior to getting myself into this mess, Sharon, a doctor in the "Class of '93" who got that embarrassing email message I meant to send to a friend, had asked me to contact her if I was ever looking for work. Sharon was the chair of a department in the Medical School at UH. I gave her a call, thinking, *why not be in touch with someone in a hiring position who overlooks foolish mistakes?* Sharon quickly created a position for me, and I left the all-one-team-minus-that-useless-instructional-designer of Teams Work to return to UH with a newfound acceptance of its downsides.

Lessons Learned
- The business world isn't for everyone.
- As in life, there are trade-offs in the workplace (e.g., while working in a slow-paced university tries my patience, being any part of a fast-paced place that exists solely for profit leaves me cold).
- Paying attention to the lessons learned on your jobs helps you avoid making the same mistakes.

Purpose, Position, People, Place, Price

- I championed my purpose straight back to higher education.
- Never again will I hold a corporate position.
- I was ready to flee the team and jump overboard for one last outdoor swim.
- An expanse of cubicles in a corporate culture was not for me.
- The salary was nice, but my corporate-revulsion-meter worked overtime.

Song Titles Inspired by the Job

- Process Champion This
- All-One-Team Lifeboat Blues

Chapter 13:

Anesthesiology Residency Educator

Ahhhhh, I was back at UH where nobody would ask me to champion any processes, and not because they didn't think I had market value, but because they had no idea why I was there. Every other person in my new department was either a doctor or a secretary. If you weren't dressed in scrubs, you'd be asked to make coffee.

The position created for me by the department chair, Sharon, was to formalize education for anesthesiology residents. As it was, the residents watched the anesthesiology faculty until they were ready to try a procedure on their own. This 'watch me, watch me, watch me, OK, now you try' method needed improvement.

The first week on this job was grim and I felt like a fish out of water, flopping around on a lonely isthmus between a pond of doctors and a pool of secretaries. I worked behind the closed door of my tiny windowless office, avoiding being asked to sharpen more pencils while studying accreditation requirements for anesthesiology residencies. Preparing the department for accreditation was part of my job, a daunting task for someone without any medical training who was busy memorizing which doctors liked cream or sugar.

The second week on the job, Sharon asked me to observe the interaction between faculty and residents in the operating rooms for a *year* before recommending any changes to the status quo. When she first suggested the idea I was intrigued, not to mention relieved to be able to wear scrubs and no longer be expected to distribute the office mail.

But being in scrubs also came with certain assumptions, and I kept my head down, avoiding eye contact with everyone in the operating rooms so I wouldn't be handed any medical instruments or internal organs. There was no place to hide in the cramped operating rooms, and there were so many vital wires and machines to avoid flopping over.

You might remember that at the age of eighteen I was an untrained, squeamish round-the-clock nurse. Taking in the sights and smells of surgery was also hard to swallow, as was witnessing that the surgery residents were on the same informal 'watch me, watch me, watch me, OK, now you try' plan as the anesthesiology residents. While observing the removal of a brain tumor, I overheard an experienced surgeon say to a surgery resident, "Oh, don't cut there!"

Observing routines and interactions in the O.R. was fascinating. When a surgeon entered the room, he stood still with his arms out for the nearest underling to dress him in a surgical jacket, like an obedient toddler when he sees his mother holding his winter coat. The next order of business was often which radio station the surgeon wanted on the dial. The choice was usually the local classic rock station, and there was much humming, singing, and chatting during operations.

For some reason I expected to be able to hear a pin drop and feel the concentration. Instead, there's much truth to what they say about a surgeon being like a mechanic, although mechanics pick up their own tools. How could everyone be so nonchalant? I just stayed quiet in the corner, realizing I couldn't possibly handle watching operations for a year when one week of it was more than enough.

Sharon recognized I was in a difficult position; being crouched in corners is uncomfortable. She graciously accepted my two-week notice of resignation, which I gave only two weeks after I'd started a job she created for me. I spent the second half of my tenure in the Anesthesiology Department outlining a preparation plan for accreditation, making one small contribution before I left, in addition to those scalpel-sharp pencils.

Lessons Learned
- Some positions (e.g., doctor or secretary) are

understood by everyone, whereas others (e.g., residency educator) are not.

- When there is something about you that isn't fitting into a workplace–the proverbial round peg that doesn't fit into the square hole–it's better to move on than it is to try to be square.
- Putting time and effort into finding suitable positions is smarter than accepting the first opportunity that comes along.

Purpose, Position, People, Place, Price

- My purpose was misunderstood.
- I can't be in a bloody position.
- Having no co-workers doing similar work was isolating.
- Operating rooms and hospitals aren't my scene.
- At least I didn't pay the price of wasting anyone's time, mine or theirs.

Song Titles Inspired by the Job

- Scrubs Made Me a Doctor
- Oh, Don't Cut There
- Fish Out of Bloody Water

Chapter 14:

Distance-Learning Consultant

When I first returned to UH I bumped into Katie, a woman I knew who directed distance learning and instructional technology for the Information Technology Division. Once back on her feet (I bumped into her hard), Katie expressed her surprise to see me back on campus. I explained why I left Teams Work and what I was facing and trying to stomach in the Anesthesiology Department. An angel who had appeared with a job, Katie rocked it with a few tunes on her harp while encouraging me to apply for a position in her department. Soon after, I stripped off the surgical scrubs to become a consultant in the Information Technology Division.

Position descriptions weren't a priority in my new department, and as it turned out, neither was pest control. (We were crammed in an old, decrepit building packed with cubicles and crawling with cockroaches and mice.) Every person in my unit created a job that matched his strengths and passions, be they gamification, video production, web design, or *playing* games and watching videos on the web. A rare work treat, I was able to create a position around my experience and interest in online education.

My top priority and main source of motivation on the job was to serve as a consultant. Any of the thousands of faculty and academic staff at UH who might be interested in distance learning could meet with me for a free one-hour consultation, which ate up about seven meaningful hours of my time over two otherwise uninspired years.

The first year on this job was pretty relaxed and we all did what we wanted and considered useful. Then a tracking and billing system was hoisted upon us, along with a requirement to bill a certain number of hours against funded projects. In the year 2000, there wasn't much funding for distance learning to support my made-up position at the Information Technology Division.

During my second year, I had to scramble to earn my keep. I became the lead trainer for UH's first online learning-management system. And, with more than a hint of satisfaction after my experiences with Dean Kaushon, I contracted with the School of Education to help them design their first online degree program.

As I was about to begin my third year in this position, I realized I needed to escape the cold heartland for the winter. My husband, John, worked with his employer to find a work-based research assignment at an environmental agency in Australia. I had banked almost enough vacation hours at UH to cover the three winter months with John in

Australia, and I was fortunate to be able to keep my job at UH.

I was short on vacation time by only 40 hours, the amount of time I could spend on professional development. Katie went for my idea to spend the 40 hours independently learning the skills needed to create interactive web sites. The final product was a multimedia web site about our adventures in Australia. You might find recording adorable Aussie children talk about a platypus irrelevant to the work I was doing for UH, but if having fun while developing new work skills is wrong, who wants to be right?

Before we returned from Australia, Katie began my performance review, a process that was past due. She was determined to get this done as soon as possible and scheduled a meeting with me my first day back to work. I worried she'd realized in my absence that nobody was knocking on my distance-learning door and that my days of playing games and watching videos on the web would soon be over.

Luckily, I had something else lined up if what Katie wanted to talk with me about was the lack of funding to keep me on staff. Shortly before I returned from Australia, the leader of online instruction in the Engineering School invited me by email to join his team to design and develop online degree programs.

Katie: Great to hear about your time down under.

Now, let's chat about work time. I realize finding funding has been challenging for you.

Me: Definitely, which makes me wonder if our department will start funding online instruction, so I don't need to contract with other departments?

Katie: That's doubtful.

Me: The Engineering School is making great strides. In fact, I've been offered a job there.

Katie: If I were in your boxy-toed shoes and wanted to stop looking for funding, I'd look into that offer.

I took her advice and left the Information Technology Division, after two years of being the primary contact for distance learning at the university, featuring seven hours of consulting and countless sightings of cockroaches and mice.

After reading the past few chapters you might be thinking, wow, what a job jumper! Well, you're right. But job jumping isn't wrong. It's a normal part of the mucky process of finding fitting work. Follow the lesson from my time at Presentations Matter and give back to each employer. Then, if the fit between you and an employer isn't right, jump away.

Lessons Learned
- Professional development is essential and can be fun.

- Short breaks from the work routine are rejuvenating.

Purpose, Position, People, Place, Price
- Meaning was found in training and consulting with instructors.
- Being a lead trainer and instructional designer was a great position.
- I connected with colleagues and had some laughs.
- The pest-infested cubicle was bad, but the location on campus was good.
- Low-priority work comes with a price.

Song Titles Inspired by the Job
- Katie's Rocking Harp
- Nobody is Knock Knock Knockin' on My Distance-Learning Door

Part D:

Working with Purpose *Plus*

Knowing the kinds of positions, people, places, and perks important in your work life helps you clarify your work purpose. Every work experience can shed light on what matters to you, illuminating your path to work with "purpose *plus*."

Chapter 15:

Instructional Designer

Although I'd done some instructional design in most of my professional positions, starting at Presentations Matter, the job in the Engineering School at UH was the only one where instructional design was my sole focus. What the instructional designer could and couldn't do was brought more into focus with each passing day by the hot-headed, territorial individuals I worked with in the Engineering School.

I was only able to take this group's heat by regularly redirecting my attention to the cool lake I could see out the wall of windows in my luxurious office. Not only did I leave behind a pest-infested cubicle for this incredible office and view, but my new workplace was a conference facility with a swimming pool and sauna. Things were looking up in so many ways, but oh my, the *people*.

My new work group was full of characters with carefully guarded roles and strong opinions, yet our director aimed to lead by consensus. Getting this motley crew to reach consensus on anything was like opening a can of argumentative worms. We were all too loud and proud, myself included. If this group sounds like the one you're working with now, run for the hills, find a quiet spot, and polish up your resume.

A couple of weeks after I began this job I was working with an instructor who wanted the handful of items in his online course menu alphabetized. I helped him make the change on the spot. As soon as I returned to the office, I got a phone call from an irate co-worker, Lucy.

Lucy: Did you just alphabetize Jay's course menu?

Me: Yes, I was meeting with him and he asked me to do that.

Lucy: Do NOT touch the course sites. That's MY job. I'm on my way to your office to talk about this.

Huh? Now I really was confused. I thought the course sites were my responsibility, and why get so bent outta shape about the same few menu items being presented in another order? Good thing Lucy stormed over from her office a few blocks away to slap my hands and clear that up. And, good thing I'd seen Lucy's type before–in Eileen, my micro manager at Upscale Retailer and Anne, the large-and-in-charge bookkeeper at the beer distributor. I try to remind myself that at work, the more you can roll with your own and others' quirks, the more at peace you'll be.

Not long after I started this job, when it came time to switch to an advanced learning-management system and create more online programs, I was free to rethink everything about the courses. I dove into the work with gusto and was hooked. I always know I am onto something in my search for work with "purpose *plus*" when my interest is sustained, which never happened as a cashier, security guard, or process champion.

There's always a catch or tradeoff with every job, though, isn't there? On this job, the catch was my values didn't align with the content of the courses I was asked to design. I tried promoting courses in sustainable engineering, such as green building or alternative energy sources, but my ideas fell silent on dirty, deaf ears (from all the gas, oil, and loud machinery handled by the mechanical engineers I worked with on courses about internal combustion engines).

In the end, the old boys' network that kept women in the department down led me to find my way out. My department was split by gender; most of the men were program directors and most of the women were program assistants. And most of what the women in the department said fell silent on the dirty, deaf ears of the old boys in charge.

I worked in the Engineering School for eight years because the work itself was inspiring; I was able to work from home when I wasn't in my lovely office with a lake view or interested in a swim; and I had a very flexible schedule. Once I started appreciating the benefits of working from home, the transition from being an employee at UH to freelancing came naturally, and I've been enjoying being my own boss ever since. Granted, I do miss that view and pool.

Lessons Learned
- Be sensitive to and learn your co-workers' roles when you begin a job. (Some people get super wiggy when they think you're stepping on their little piggy.)
- Doing work you value is important.

Purpose, Position, People, Place, Price
- I really got and stayed in the zone with meaningful, challenging work.
- This was a great position to hold onto, if you're a man.
- Old boys as the only leaders and a dysfunctional team were a bad combination.
- The downtown vibe and my office with a lake view and pool were awesome.
- Paying the price of womanhood got old, old boys.

Song Titles Inspired by the Job
- Work Groove
- Loud Proud Crowd

Chapter 16:

First Mate

John and I were yearning for another international getaway and winter escape, this time a longer one that landed us for a year in Bristol, a city of half a million people in Southern England. John completed a fellowship and I took a leave of absence from UH, but I had some laughs and covered my personal expenses working on water.

My job was first mate on a commuter ferry that ran 40-minute loops around Bristol Harbor, a body of water that starts in the City Centre and stretches over a mile to our old neighborhood, Hotwells. The ferry stopped at several pubs, restaurants, and other points of interest on the route. The skipper, Rich, was a native Bristolian with a telltale accent to anyone who's lived there. Rich was a modern-day pirate, playing the part in every way, especially when opening his mouf (Bristolians pronounce "th" like "f"). I still smile every time I fink of Rich.

I became friends with Rich through Hannah, Rich's wife and John's fellowship mentor at the environment agency in Bristol. John and I were invited to a work party, where everyone from the agency was drinking pints of beer and talking shop. Since Rich and I weren't part of the shop, we drank and talked about all things Bristolian. After a few hours of fun banter, Rich asked if I'd be his first mate every other Sunday during the winter months. I took the job without any idea of what was involved, which turned out to be a short list of duties:

1. watch for and alert Rich when people want on or off the ferry;
2. jump off and tie up the ferry at stops;
3. push off and hop in the ferry when ready to go;
4. help people on and off the ferry;
5. collect fares;
6. keep the seats dry;
7. update the "Next Ferry" time on chalkboards; and
8. buy cigarettes and various sundries for Rich in the City Centre, where each loop around the harbor began and ended.

I'd also say, "Mind the gap," a very British and absolutely necessary expression given there actually was a nerve-wracking, gaping divide between the top of Rich's rickety step stool and the best place to enter his tugboat-shaped ferry. Parents would hand me babies who, had they slipped through my hands, would've landed straight in the water without a single snag to their swaddling clothes.

Being the worrier I am, I asked Rich what I should do if anyone fell overboard. He pointed to a hook he'd duct taped to a wobbly stick, rather than splurging for a functional life-saving device, while reassuring me nobody but drunk people on pub crawls ever fell overboard; since I was working on Sunday afternoons, we wouldn't see as much of that.

Rich owned two ferries but only operated both on busy spring and summer days. I worked one day in the spring and had a once in a lifetime experience as the first mate for the skipper, Glen, on Rich's second ferry. Glen was from Glasgow and had such a thick Scottish accent I literally couldn't understand most of the words he said.

Glen: Saklj wiotru lkjsf aklrjt.

Me: Sorry, did you say you're ready for me to push off?

Glen: Saklj wiotru lkjsf aklrjt.

Me: Was that stop at the train station?

Glen: Saklj wiotru lkjsf aklrjt!

Me: Tie up here, then?

This went on all day as I awkwardly tried to navigate a new ferry route that brought people to the train station, which meant I couldn't overlook people on a schedule waiting at stops I wasn't aware of until decoding Glen's exaggerated points and grunts. As Rich would recount, there were a lot of hand gestures and indecipherable grunts coming out of all our moufs that day.

After 13 years, Rich tired of driving circles around a floating harbor and sold his ferry business to find other work for pirates. I was bored after 13 hours, but the novelty of working wif a lively local was great fun.

Lessons Learned

- Jobs can come in many shapes and sizes.
- Communicate with co-workers, whatever it takes.

Purpose, Position, People, Place, Price

- This was a fun life experience–no more, no less.
- The duties were simple, when the skipper and I spoke the same language.
- I loved working for a spirited pirate and with locals.
- Being on the water was novel and entertaining.
- There was no price to pay, other than low pay.

Song Titles Inspired by the Job

- Circles of Time
- Mind the Deathtrap Gap
- Saklj Wiotru Lkjsf Aklrjt

Chapter 17:

Independent Contractor

I left a highly coveted and compensated position with UH at the height of a recession to launch my own business. Friends and colleagues thought I was nuts, but I knew staying put was my way down to crazy town. More importantly, I'd learned enough to take a risk and I was motivated to become a freelance instructional designer.

My first client was a penny-pinching acupuncturist. Dr. Chan also ran a massage school, and he hired me to create a program in massage therapy that combined weekends of hands-on training with online instruction. I wrote a detailed plan for the accrediting body of Dr. Chan's school, and we got straight to work when told if we stuck with the plan, our proposed program would be accredited.

As was obvious in everything from the cracked, faux leather furniture and flimsy massage tables to students doing the lion's share of the office work as part of the "massage curriculum," Dr. Chan followed his one and only plan: cut corners and trim dollars wherever possible. I've never seen such a massaged curriculum. The accrediting body rescinded approval based on Dr. Chan's first progress report, which included evidence that he'd already short-changed the plan and that I needed to find another acupuncturist and client.

I struck gold and made a friend in my next client, Margie, a director of online learning at another large, public university in the heartland that I'll call UH2. A couple of years prior, Margie had attended a workshop I gave at UH and asked if I ever consulted on the side. I kept her card and contacted her after leaving UH and cheap Dr. Chan.

Margie told me my timing was perfect because she had an immediate need. My first project at UH2 was to design an online graduate course in finance within a month. The instructor had never taught online, but we got the job done. Next came another new course for me to frantically design and produce quickly with another inexperienced instructor, trailed by several more of the stressful same–until I had proven myself and could ease into a relaxed mix of course timelines and lower my blood pressure.

Fast-forwarding to today and tying all of the dimensions at work together, I have a position and company I created to work part-time from home, exactly where I want to be. I appreciate that my work as an educator is meaningful, varied, flexible, autonomous, and challenging, and that my clients are smart, funny, and innovative. An experienced professional, I can finally name my "price" without selling my soul. Every day I relish the simple pleasures of being my own boss, such as wearing sweatpants to virtual meetings. (Other meeting participants can only see my head and shoulders).

It took me a long time to arrive here because where I was going was not always clear. That said, had I been more reflective along the way or come up with the dimensions of purpose, position, people, place and price sooner, I wouldn't have enough silly stories for a book.

Lessons Learned

- Being your own boss is fantastic.
- When it comes to the workplace, there's no place like home.

Purpose, Position, People, Place, Price

- My purpose as an educator is met and the work is meaningful.
- Combining teaching, instructional design, and production work is ideal.
- I'm my own boss and choose my clients, all of whom are good people.
- Dorothy from "The Wizard of Oz" was so right.
- Now seasoned, I can name my price and I no longer have to pay any price.

Song Titles Inspired by the Job

- Boss of Me

- Autonomy Now

Parting Thoughts

I hope you've laughed and learned while reading my stories. Looking back on my own journey, I've come to believe that finding humor in the absurd moments of any given job is critical to getting something positive out of the experience. And it's good to be able to laugh at yourself. It might even spawn a book.

www.ingramcontent.com/pod-product-compliance
Lightning Source LLC
Chambersburg PA
CBHW070536030426
42337CB00016B/2233